D1536449

Presented by:

_____

To:

_____

Date:

_____

Occasion:

_____

The Path
of Merciful Love

"99 Words to Live By"

A series of fine gift books that offers the inspirational words of well-known spiritual figures as well as proverbs from many cultures and traditions, exploring topics that have moved and will continue to move many people's hearts. Perfect for daily reflection as well as moments of relaxation.

The Path
of Merciful Love

99 Sayings
by Thérèse of Lisieux

edited by
Marc Foley, O.C.D.

New City Press
Hyde Park, NY

Published in the United States by New City Press
202 Cardinal Rd., Hyde Park, NY 12538
©2006 The Discalced Carmelites of the Immaculate
        Heart of Mary Province

Cover design by Leandro De Leon

Library of Congress Cataloging-in-Publication Data:

Thérèse, de Lisieux, Saint, 1873-1897
    [Selections. English. 2006]
    The path of merciful love: 99 sayings / by Thérèse
    of Lisieux; edited by Marc Foley.
        p. cm.
      ISBN-13: 978-1-56548-245-6 (alk. paper)
      ISBN-10: 1-56548-245-X (alk. paper)
    1. Meditations. 2. Catholic Church--Prayer-books and de-
votions--English. I. Foley, Marc, 1949- II. Title. III. Series.
    BX4700.T5A25 2006
    242--dc22   2006005494

Printed in the United States of America

Thérèse of Lisieux is an enigma. She was born in an upper middle-class bourgeois family in Alençon, France, in 1873, lived a sheltered childhood, an uneventful, cloistered adulthood, and in obscurity died of tuberculosis at the age of twenty-four; yet her appeal is universal. Social activist Dorothy Day, agnostic playwright and novelist Georges Bernanos, beat-poets Allen Ginsberg and Jack Kerovac, café singer Edith Piaf, theologian Hans Urs von Balthasar, Jewish philosopher Henri Bergson, are but a few examples of diverse people who have testified to the influence of Saint Thérèse in their lives.

When Thérèse was dying, one of the nuns in the Lisieux Carmel said, "Sister Thérèse will die soon; what will Mother Prioress be able to write about her in her obituary? She entered our convent, lived and died. There is nothing else that can be said. We cannot even say that she was a good religious, for we never saw her practicing virtue." Yet, Saint Pius X called this same "mediocre" nun the greatest saint of modern times. She has been named co-patroness of France and the missions and declared a Doctor of the Universal Church by Pope John Paul II (a distinction conferred on only thirty-three saints in the history of the Church).

Saint Thérèse, who lived and died in anonymity, is one of the most well-known and beloved saints of our age. Her spiritual autobiography, *Story of a Soul*, has been translated into nearly sixty languages and has nourished countless people with a message that everyone finds accessible.

Thérèse's message is not new, for the core concepts of her spirituality are rooted in the Gospel —

love, mercy, trust, and surrender. But she presents these perennial verities in a fresh and appealing manner. Thérèse related to God as an innocent child, full of trust and devoid of fear, for she looked upon God as a loving parent. This was a radical departure from the spirituality of her day that emphasized the depravity of human nature and the harsh justice of God. In contrast, the core of Thérèse's "Little Way" to holiness "is the abandonment of the little child who sleeps without fear in his Father's arms."

Thérèse taught that sanctity is within everyone's grasp, for we are "made holy by the practice of the hidden virtues, the ordinary virtues," especially the virtue of love. For Thérèse love was not a feeling but a choice. Sometimes the choice to love required self-sacrifice. But Thérèse did not consider self-sacrifice a joyless obligation, for she discovered that when she could forget herself in order to love her neighbor, she became truly happy.

Thérèse's happiness was not devoid of pain and conflict, however, for her cloistered existence was a "martyrdom of pinpricks," the daily aggravations and annoyances that are part and parcel of living in close quarters with the same people day in and day out. Precisely in this fact does her life mirror our own. Saint Thérèse can teach us how to find God in the mundaneness of daily life.

Marc Foley, O.C.D.

God willed to create great souls comparable to lilies and roses. But he has created smaller ones and these must be content to be daisies or violets destined to give joy to God's glances. Perfection consists in doing God's will, in being what he wills us to be.

It seems to me that if a little flower could speak, it would tell simply what God has done for it without trying to hide its blessings. It would not say, under the pretext of a false humility, it is not beautiful or without perfume.

Upon examining the contents of a kaleidoscope (bits of straw, paper, etc.):

So long as our actions, even the most trivial remain within love's kaleidoscope, the Blessed Trinity imparts to them a marvelous brightness and beauty.... The eye-piece of the spy-glass symbolizes the good God who, looking from the outside (but through himself, as it were) into the kaleidoscope, finds everything quite beautiful, even our miserable straws of effort and our most insignificant actions.

Can a father scold his child when the child owns up to its fault? Certainly not. It is like a king on a hunt, who noticed his dogs pursuing a white rabbit. When the rabbit sensed that the dogs were about to pounce on him, the rabbit bounded into the arms of the King. Deeply moved by this show of confidence, the king cherished the rabbit thereafter as his own.... This is how God will treat us if we are hunted down by the claims of Divine Justice, represented by the dogs in the story, if we run for refuge into the very arms of our Judge.

Once a lord built a church with his name carved on the cornerstone. The next day the only name on the stone was that of an unknown woman. The Lord restored his name but the same phenomenon happened again. The unknown name was found to belong to a poor woman who, during the construction of the church, spent her last coin to buy hay for the horses who were dragging heavy loads of stone, reasoning, "I cannot contribute to the building of this temple, but God may accept my offering." The humbled lord understood and left her name on the cornerstone. The least action inspired by love is of greater merit than the most outstanding achievement.

It is the spirit of gratitude which draws down upon us the overflow of God's grace, for no sooner have we thanked God for one blessing than he hastens to send ten additional favors in return.... For a grace received faithfully, God granted me a multitude of others.

Have you ever noticed that normally most of us are quite willing to *give* with a generous hand? But not to allow others *to take away* what belongs to us!

Oh! the unfathomable tenderness of God's exquisite mercy towards the weak.... I marvel how God always surrounds them with his protecting love. We should act in the same way toward our neighbor. Even in nature we have a faint image of this provident concern when we compare the coarse bean with the little green pea. Although both must endure the heat of the day and the chill of the night, the attractive pea has not received the extra protection of the tough outer covering of the unattractive bean. In imitation of our Heavenly Father, let us bestow a more indulgent love and protective care on those who have the greater need.

Thérèse's response to a nun who complained about having been interrupted in her work by a request from another nun:

At the moment of death,
such an interruption
will be seen
in a very different light.
You will thank God for it.

Advice given to a novice who used to avoid passing the infirmary so that she would not be asked to do something:

You should purposely pass the infirmary to give the sick sisters an opportunity to ask services which might inconvenience you. And if at times you cannot carry out their request, tell them so in an amiable way and promise to return. You should show a cheerful attitude about all this in order to make your patients believe that they are doing you a favor in accepting your services.

There are things
the heart feels
but which the tongue
and even the mind
cannot express.

Once I was surprised that God didn't give equal glory to all the Elect in heaven, and I was afraid all would not be perfectly happy. So my sister Pauline filled a large tumbler and a thimble to the brim with water and asked me which one was fuller. I told her each was as full as the other and that it was impossible to put in more water than they could contain. I then understood that in heaven God will grant his Elect as much glory as they can take, the last having nothing to envy in the first.

I feel that it is far more valuable to speak *to* God than to speak about Him, for there is so much self-love intermingled with spiritual conversations.

True courage does not consist in those momentary ardors which impel us to go out and win the world for Christ — at the cost of imaginable danger, which only adds another touch of romance to our beautiful dreams. No, the courage that counts with God is that type of courage which our Lord showed in the Garden of Olives; on the one hand, a natural desire to turn away from suffering; on the other hand, in anguish of soul, the willingness to accept the chalice which his Father had sent him.

The goal
of all our undertakings
should not be
a task perfectly completed
but the accomplishment
of the will of God.

While walking in the garden in the Lisieux Carmel, to a novice:

Those pears are not attractive now. But in the fall, when they are stewed and served in the refectory, we shall find them to our taste, and it will be hard to connect them with the fruit which we are looking at now. This is a good reminder of the truth that on the Last Day ... those Sisters, whose natural qualities may now be displeasing to us, might appear to us as great saints. And we shall perhaps gaze on them open-mouthed in wonder.

I felt *charity*
enter into my soul,
and the need
to forget myself
and to please others;
since then
I've been happy.

On a train ride through the Alps:

When I saw the beauty of the Alps, very profound thoughts came to life in my soul. I seemed to understand the grandeur of God and the marvels of heaven. Religious life appeared to me *exactly as it is* with its small sacrifices carried out in the shadows. I understood how easy it is to become all wrapped up in self, forgetting the sublime goal of one's calling. I said to myself: When I am in Carmel and trials come my way and I have only a tiny bit of the starry heavens to contemplate, I shall remember what my eyes have seen today. This will encourage me and I shall easily forget my own little interests, recalling the grandeur and power of God, this God whom alone I want to love.

Joy isn't found
in the material objects
surrounding us
but in the inner recesses
of the soul.
One can possess joy
in a prison cell
as well as in a palace.

Living on Love
is giving without limit.
Living on Love
is banishing every fear.

If I think about tomorrow,
I fear my fickleness.
I feel sadness and worry
rising up in my heart.
But I'm willing, my God,
to accept trial and suffering
just for today.

Prayer and sacrifice
can touch souls much better
than words.

I love to recite prayers in common ... but when I am alone (and I am ashamed to admit it) the recitation of the rosary is more difficult for me than the wearing of an instrument of penance.... I force myself in vain to meditate on the mysteries of the rosary; I don't succeed in fixing my mind on them. For a long time I was desolate about this lack of devotion.... Now I am less desolate; I think that the Queen of heaven, since she is *my MOTHER,* must see my good will and she is satisfied with it.

Great is the power of *prayer*. One could call it a Queen who has at each instant free access to the King and who is able to obtain whatever she asks. To be heard, it is not necessary to read from a book some beautiful formula composed for the occasion.... I pray like children who do not know how to read, I say very simply to God what I wish to say, without composing beautiful sentences, and he always understands me. For me, *prayer* is an aspiration of the heart, it is a simple glance directed to heaven, it is a cry of gratitude and love in the midst of trial as well as joy; finally, it is something great, supernatural, which expands my soul and unites me to Jesus.

Jesus *has forgiven me more* than St. Mary Magdalene. He forgave me *in advance* by preventing me from falling. Suppose that a clever physician's child trips over a stone and breaks a limb. His father cares for his hurt. His child, completely cured, shows his gratitude. But, if the father knows of the stone in his child's way and removes it without the child's knowledge, though he is the object of his father's tender foresight, he will *love him less*, than if he had been cured by his father, for he does not know what his father has done. If he discovers the danger from which he has escaped, *will he not love his father more?* I am this child, the object of God's *foreseeing love*, who has not sent his Word to save the *just* but *sinners*.

God
is pleased to show
his goodness and power
by using the least
worthy instruments.

God stretches out
his *hand* to ask,
his hand is never *empty*,
and his intimate friends
can draw from him
the courage and strength
they need.

You must become gentle;
never any harsh words,
never a harsh tone;
never take on a harsh look,
always be gentle.

On a pilgrimage to Rome:

Having never lived among the great of this world, Céline and I found ourselves in the midst of the nobility who almost exclusively made up the pilgrimage. Ah! far from dazzling us, all these titles appeared to us as nothing but smoke. From a distance, this had sometimes thrown a little powder in my eyes, but close up, I saw that "all that glistens is not gold," and I understood the words of *The Imitation of Christ*, "Be not solicitous for the shadow of a great name." I understood true greatness is to be found in *the soul*, not in a *name*.

The closer
one approaches God,
the simpler
one becomes.

I should feel desolate for having slept for seven years during my hours of prayer and my thanksgivings after Holy Communion; well I am not desolate. I remember that *little children* are as pleasing to their parents when they are asleep as when they are wide awake.

Mother Geneviève was made holy by the practice of the hidden virtues, the ordinary virtues. Ah! that type of sanctity seems the *truest* and the *most holy* to me, and it is the type that I desire because in it one meets with no deceptions.

I understood
that without *love*
all works are nothing,
even the most dazzling,
such as raising the dead
to life or converting people.

How sweet is the way of *love*. True, one can fall or commit infidelities but, knowing *how to draw profit from everything*, love quickly consumes everything that can be displeasing to Jesus; it leaves nothing but a humble and profound peace in the depths of the heart.

Jesus has no need of books or teachers to instruct souls; he teaches without the noise of words. Never have I heard him speak, but I feel that he is within me at each moment; he is guiding and inspiring me with what I must say and do.

It seems to me that if all creatures had received the same graces I received, God would be feared by none but would be loved to the point of folly.

I understand that all souls cannot be the same, that it is necessary there be different types in order to honor each of God's perfections in a particular way.

God's justice ... seems to me clothed in *love*. What a sweet joy it is to think that God is *just*, i.e., that he takes into account our weakness, that he is perfectly aware of our fragile nature. What should I fear then?

I have no way of proving my love for you other than that of strewing of flowers, that is, not allowing one little sacrifice to escape, not one look, one word, profiting by all the smallest things and doing them through love.

I only love simplicity;
I have a horror for pretense.

Concerning an emotionally ill nun:

I assure you I have the greatest compassion for Sister Marie of St. Joseph. If you knew her as well as I do, you would see that she is not responsible for all of the things that seem so awful to us.... She is to be pitied! She is like an old clock that has to be re-wound every quarter of an hour. Yes, it is as bad as that. I remind myself that if I had as defective a spirit as she does, I would not do any better, and then I would despair.... Oh, how necessary it is to practice charity toward one's neighbor.

Shortly after working for a full year with Sr. Marie of St. Joseph:

This year God has given me the grace to understand what charity is; I understood it before ... but in an imperfect way. Until this year I never fathomed the meaning of these words of Jesus: *"The second commandment is LIKE the first: You shall love your neighbor as yourself."* Ah! I understood now that charity consists in bearing with the faults of others, in not being surprised at their weakness, in being edified by the smallest acts of virtue we see them practice.... Charity must not remain hidden in the bottom of the heart ... *but placed on the lampstand, so as to give light to ALL in the house.... ALL in the house without distinction.*

In response to a novice who admitted to Thérèse that she envied her good works:

If our wretchedness causes us too much suffering, we must offer to God other people's good works. That's one of the benefits of the communion of saints. … For if I love the good that is in my neighbor as much as he loves it himself, that good is as much mine as it is his. Through this communion I can enrich myself with all the good there is in heaven and on earth, in the angels, in the saints and in all those who love God.

In response to a novice's frustration with her inability to overcome her impatience with certain members of the community:

If you are that easily overcome, it is because you do not soften your heart in advance. When you are exasperated with someone, the way to recover your peace of mind is to pray for that person.

Having noticed the infirmarian softening the linen to give her some relief from suffering:

People must be treated with the same care. How often we hurt them without realizing it! Many people are sick, others are weak, and all of them are suffering. We ought to be very gentle with them. One should always treat others charitably, for very often what we think is negligence is heroic in God's eyes. A sister who is suffering from migraine or is troubled internally does more when she does half of what is required of her than another who does it all but is sound in mind and body.

You probably think that I do as I say. No, I am not always faithful, but I am never discouraged. I drop into the arms of Jesus.... It is enough to bear one's faults meekly; that is true holiness.... When we accept our disappointment at our failures, God immediately returns to us.

During her night of faith:

If you only knew what darkness I am plunged into! I don't believe in eternal life; I think that after this life there is nothing.... God knows very well that while I do not have *the joy of faith*, I am trying to carry out its works at least.... When I sing of the happiness of heaven and of the eternal possession of God, I feel no joy in this, for I sing simply what I WANT TO BELIEVE.

Let us see life
as it really is.
It is a moment
between two eternities.

I have seen for myself that often the nuns who apparently have the strongest natures are those most easily overcome in little things — so true it is that the greatest of victories is the conquest of self.

Sometimes it happens that despite their best efforts, God allows some souls to remain imperfect because it would be to their spiritual detriment to believe they are virtuous.

Charity
consists in bearing
with those who
are unbearable.

Suffering unbearable pain because of her tuberculosis:

Pray for those who are sick and dying.... If you only knew what goes on! How little it takes to lose control of oneself!... What a grace it is to have faith! If I had no faith, I would have inflicted death on myself without hesitating a moment!... I'm surprised that there are not more atheists who commit suicide!

Everything
is a grace.

Love knows
how to draw profit
from everything;
from the good
and from the bad
that is found in us.

I have a lot of distractions during prayer, but as soon as I
perceive them I pray for the
persons that occupy my imagi-
nation and this way they benefit
from my distractions.

God has two weaknesses that make him lovable. He is blind … and he doesn't know arithmetic! his love makes him perfectly blind. For when the greatest sinner on earth repents at the moment of death and dies in an act of love, God does not count either the numerous graces that the sinner has abused or his crimes but counts only his last prayer and receives him without any delay into his merciful arms.

The only true beauty that exists is holiness. There is no other! A virtuous person, however ugly she might be, has a charm one can't resist; conversely, a person with looks but without virtue is as disagreeable as can be!

It is amazing how easily souls lose peace when it comes to the virtue of purity!... The means of being freed from these temptations is to regard them with calm, not to be astonished, much less to fear them.... It is exactly this fear, this discouragement, that the devil takes advantage of in order to make souls fall. However, one temptation of pride is by far more dangerous — and God is much more offended when we yield to that — than when one commits a fault, even a grave one, against purity.... Pride, however, is a fault that souls often commit easily without being upset!

Keep in mind the method used to make copper objects shine. You smear them with mud after which they will shine like gold. Temptations are like mud for the soul. They serve to make the virtues, which are opposed to these temptations, to shine forth.

When you feel too weak to pick up a ball of yarn and you do it anyway for the love of Jesus, you have more merit than if you had accomplished something much more important in a moment of fervor. Instead of being sad when you get to feel your weakness, rejoice that God is providing you with the opportunity to save a greater number of souls for him!... What a grace when in the morning we feel no strength to practice virtue ... in one act of love, even *unfelt* love, all is repaired.

To a novice who failed to show gratitude:

You must get used to letting your gratitude be seen, to say thank you with an open heart for the least little thing.... Otherwise, your lack of expressing gratitude will freeze your heart and destroy cordiality that is necessary in community.

When the devil tries to place before the eyes of my soul the faults of such and such a sister who is less attractive to me, I hasten to search out her virtues, her good intentions; I tell myself that even if I did see her fall once, she could easily have won a great number of victories which she is hiding through humility, and that even what appears to me as a fault can very easily be an act of virtue because of her intention. I have no trouble in convincing myself of this truth because of a little experience I had which showed me we must never judge. *(See next saying.)*

During an unpleasant recreation, when asked whether she or a sister sitting next to her would help bring in the community Christmas tree:

I untied my apron slowly in order that my companion untie hers first, for I thought of giving her the pleasure. Seeing me get up last, the sister said, "I thought so, you are not going to gain this pearl for your crown." The community believed I had acted through selfishness. This small thing did to my soul good. It made me indulgent toward the weaknesses of others and prevented me from being vain when I am judged favorably. Since one can take my acts of virtue for imperfections, one can take for virtue what is nothing but imperfection.

There is a sister who displeases me in everything. Not wishing to give in to my natural antipathy, I told myself that charity consists not in feelings but in works. So I did for this sister what I would do for the person I loved the most. I prayed for her ... and rendered her all the services possible. But frequently ... when I worked with her, I used to run away like a deserter whenever my struggles became too violent. She was unaware of my feelings for her, she never suspected the motives for my conduct.... My *last means* of not being defeated was desertion.... My last plank of salvation was flight.

It is only charity
that can expand my heart.

From the moment I understood that it was impossible for me to do anything by myself, the task imposed upon me being novice mistress no longer appeared difficult.... If I had depended in the least on my own strength, I would very soon have had to give up.

Reflecting on some of the sisters:

There is a lack of judgment, a lack of good manners, touchiness ... all the things which don't make life agreeable. These characteristics are chronic and there is no hope for a cure.... But I also know that my Mother would not cease to take care of me, to try to console me, if I remained sick all my life. This is the conclusion I draw from this: I must seek out ... the company of sisters who are the least agreeable to me in order to carry out with regard to these wounded souls the office of the good Samaritan. A word, an amiable smile often suffice to make a sad soul bloom.

I once heard a story of a boarding school teacher who was praised because she was able to extricate herself cleverly from situations without offending anyone. She said to this one: "You're not wrong"; to that one: "You are right." I thought to myself: This is not good! This teacher should have had no fear and should have told her little girls that they were wrong when this was the truth. It is always so easy to place the blame on someone who is absent, and this immediately calms the one who is complaining to you. It is just the contrary with me. If I'm not loved, that's just too bad! I tell the whole truth, and if anyone doesn't wish to know the truth, let her not come looking for me.

We should never allow kindness to degenerate into weakness. When we have scolded someone with just reason, we must leave the matter there without ... tormenting ourselves for having caused pain or at seeing one suffer and cry. To run after the afflicted one to console her does more harm than good. Leaving her to herself forces her to have recourse to God in order to see her faults. Otherwise, accustomed to receiving consolation after a merited reprimand, she will always act ... like a spoiled child, stamping her feet and crying until her mother comes to dry her tears.

Commenting on Dr. De Cornière's regret at not having been allowed to perform an autopsy on a friend of hers, who had just died:

Ah! it's in this way that we are indifferent towards one another on earth! Would he say the same thing if it were a question of his own mother or sister?

In response to the prioress who, noticing a draft in the infirmary caused by an open window and door, became angry and demanded to know who had left them open:

I told Mother Prioress the truth, but while I was speaking, there came to my mind a more charitable way of expressing it than the one I was going to use…. I followed my inspiration, and God rewarded me for it with a great interior peace.

In response to the belief common in Thérèse's time that without baptism children are damned:

Little children are not damned.

Oh, what poisonous praises I've seen served up to Mother Prioress! How necessary it is for a person to be detached and elevated from herself in order not to experience any harm!

I will have the right of doing stupid things up until my death, if I am humble and if I remain little. Look at children: they never stop breaking things, tearing things, falling down, and they do this even while loving their parents very, very much.... When I fall in this way ... I say to myself: What would I do and what would I become, if I were to rely upon my own strength?

I understand why St. Peter fell.... He was relying upon himself.... I'm sure that if St. Peter had said humbly to Jesus: "Give me the grace I beg you to follow you even to death," he would have received it immediately.... And Jesus could have said to St. Peter: "Ask me for the strength to accomplish what you want." But no, he didn't because he wanted to show him his weakness and because, before ruling the Church that is filled with sinners, he had to experience for himself what man is able to do without God's help. Before Peter fell, Jesus had said to him: "And once you're converted, strengthen your brethren." This means: Convince them of the weakness of human strength through your own experience.

I'm suffering very much,
but am I suffering very well?
That's the point!

The more sacrifices cost you the more you must concentrate on making them cheerfully. Never miss an opportunity, for if only you knew the value Jesus sets on even the tiniest act of self-denial, you would grasp at every opportunity like a miser going after treasure.

The main cause of your suffering and struggles ... is that you seek your own satisfaction too much. Do you know how to find true happiness? When you don't seek your satisfaction anymore. Believe me, I know this by experience.

Jesus holds out his hand to us like a *beggar* so that on the radiant day of judgment when he will appear in his glory, he may have us hear those sweet words: "Come, blessed of my Father, for I was hungry and you gave me to eat; I was thirsty, and you gave me to drink; I did not know where to lodge, and you gave me a home, I was in prison, sick, and you helped me...." He places himself, so to speak, at our mercy, he does not want to take anything unless we give it to him, and the smallest thing is precious in his divine eyes.

To her sister Céline, on discovering that the maid she had hired to take care of her invalid father was an alcoholic:

Your poor maid is very unfortunate in having such a bad habit.... I will really pray for her; perhaps were I in her place, I would be less good than she is, and perhaps, too, she would have been already a great saint if she had received half the graces God has granted to me.

Letter to Abbé Bellière, a seminarian, who was conscripted into the army and who struggled with the temptations of army life:

Now that the storm has passed, I thank the good God for making you go through it, for we read these beautiful words in our Bible: "Happy the man who has suffered," and again: "He who has not been tempted what does he know?" In fact, when Jesus calls a person to lead a great number of others to salvation, it is very necessary that he make him experience the trials and temptations of life.

I understand
that the smallest events
of our life are conducted
by God; he is the One
who makes us desire
and who grants our desires.

If you are willing
to bear serenely
the trial of being
displeasing to yourself,
you will be ... a pleasant
place of shelter.

Letter to Abbé Bellière who is discouraged by his repeated falls into sin:

I picture a father who has two disobedient children. When he comes to punish them, he sees one of them who trembles and runs away from him in terror ... but in the bottom of his heart has the feeling that he deserves to be punished. His brother, on the contrary, throws himself into his father's arms, saying that he is sorry ... that he loves his father, and to prove it he will be good from now on.... The father realizes, however, that more than once his second son will fall into the same faults, but he is prepared to pardon him always, if his son always takes him by his heart.

To Fr. Adolphe Roulland, a missionary priest in China:

If I am alone, what consoles me is to think that at your side I can be useful for something. In fact, zero by itself has no value, but when placed next to a unit it becomes powerful, provided, however, that it is placed on the *right side*, after and not before…. That is where Jesus has placed me, and I hope to remain there always.

If we still wish to attempt doing something *great* even under the pretext of zeal, Good Jesus leaves us all alone.... It suffices to humble oneself, to bear with one's imperfections. That is real sanctity!

I have frequently noticed that after I have committed a fault my soul experiences a certain sadness or uneasiness for some time. Then I tell myself, "Now, little one, this is the price you must pay for your fault" and so I patiently bear with the trial until the little debt is paid....

I say to God: "My God, I know I have merited this feeling of sadness, but let me offer it up to you just the same as a trial that you sent me through love."

Those who
judge you unfavorably
are not robbing
you of anything.
It is they who are the losers.
For is there anything
sweeter than the inward
joy that comes from
thinking well of others?

Once when Thérèse was placing an artificial flower on the altar, a nun who could not endure any strong fragrance, approached Thérèse for the sake of reprimanding her:

At that moment, I had a strong desire to let this good nun go ahead and actually complain before telling her that it was only an artificial flower. But at that moment, Jesus was tugging at my heart for a sacrifice of this selfish satisfaction.... Holding up the flower, I exclaimed gaily: "See, sister, how well they imitate nature nowadays! Wouldn't you think that this rose had just been freshly gathered from the garden?" If you only knew how happy I was after that act of charity, and how marvelously it strengthened my character.

As little birds learn to *sing* by listening to their parents, so children learn the science of the virtues, the sublime *song* of Divine Love, from souls responsible for forming them.

On teaching her novices:

I scatter the good seed that God gives me among my little birds, and then let events take their course without worrying about the outcome. Sometimes I think I had sown nothing but God says: just go on giving and don't worry about anything else.

Written to her sister Céline on New Year's Eve, 1889:

You are the one getting my last "*adieu*" for this year!... In a few hours, it will have passed forever.... It will be in eternity.... Perhaps the year about to begin will be our last!!!! Therefore, let us profit from the shortest moments; let us act as misers.... Another year has passed! It is gone, gone and will never return, and just as this year has passed so also will our life pass and soon we shall say: "It is gone."

When the human heart gives itself to God, it loses nothing of its innate tenderness; in fact, this tenderness grows when it becomes more pure and more divine.

The desires of mothers
echo in the souls
of their children.

The most beautiful thoughts and insights are nothing without good works ... even though others can draw profit from them.... And if this soul takes delight in her *beautiful thoughts* and says the prayer of the Pharisee, she is like a person dying of hunger at a well-filled table where all his guests are enjoying abundant food.

In response to Abbé Bellière's fear that when Thérèse goes to heaven she will not be compassionate toward him because she will then be sharing in the Justice of God:

You do not understand heaven in the way that I do. It seems to you that when I die and go to heaven I would be unable to excuse your faults as I do on earth. Are you forgetting that I shall be sharing in the infinite mercy of the Lord? I believe the Blessed have great compassion on our miseries, they remember, being weak and mortal like us, they committed the same faults, sustained the same combats, and their fraternal tenderness becomes greater than it was when they were on earth, and for this reason, they never cease protecting us and praying for us. *A Dieu* dear little brother.

There are really more differences among souls than there are among faces. Therefore, it is impossible to act with all in the same manner. With certain souls, I feel I must make myself little, not fearing to humble myself by admitting my own struggles and defects.... With others, on the contrary, I have seen that to do them any good I must be very firm.... To abase oneself would not then be humility but weakness.

The graces we receive are often due to the prayers of a hidden soul. I have often thought that I may owe the graces I've received to the prayers of a person whom I shall know only in heaven. In heaven, we shall not meet with indifferent glances, for the elect will discover that they owe to each other the graces that merited their crowns.

Your Face
is my only Homeland.

Sources

Thérèse of Lisieux. *Story of a Soul*. trans. John Clarke, O.C.D. Washington, D.C.: ICS Publications, 1996.

_____. *Her Last Conversations*. trans. John Clarke, O.C.D. Washington, D.C.: ICS Publications, 1977.

_____. *Saint Thérèse of Lisieux: General Correspondence. Volume I, 1877-1890*. Trans. John Clarke, O.C.D. Washington, D.C.: ICS Publications, 1982.

_____. *Letters of Saint Thérèse of Lisieux: Volume II, 1890-1897*. Trans. John Clarke, O.C.D., Washington, D.C.: ICS Publications, 1988.

_____. *Collected Letters of Saint Thérèse of Lisieux*. Trans. F.J. Sheed. New York: Sheed & Ward, 1949.

_____. *The Poetry of Saint Thérèse of Lisieux*. trans. Donald Kinney, O.C.D. Washington, D.C.: ICS Publications, 1995.

Pierre Descouvermont, *Thérèse of Lisieux and Marie of the Trinity: The Transformative Relationship of Saint Thérèse of Lisieux and Her Novice Sister Marie of the Trinity*. Trans. Alexandra Plettenberg-Seban. New York: Alba House, 1997.

Sister Geneviève of the Holy Face (Céline Martin), *A Memoir of My Sister Saint Thérèse*. Trans. Carmelite Sisters of New York. New York: P.J. Kenedy & Sons, 1959.

Christopher O'Mahony, ed. *Saint Thérèse of Lisieux: By Those Who Knew Her, Testimonies from the Process of Beatification*. Dublin: Veritas Publications, 1975.